My Secret World

Dazzling Dolphins

Kay Woodward

Illustrated by Strawberrie Donnelly

PUFFIN

PUFFIN BOOKS

Published by the Penguin Group
Penguin Books Ltd, 80 Strand, London WC2R 0RL, England
Penguin Group (USA), Inc., 375 Hudson Street, New York, New York 10014, USA
Penguin Books Australia Ltd, 250 Camberwell Road, Camberwell,
Victoria 3124, Australia
Penguin Books Canada Ltd, 10 Alcorn Avenue, Toronto, Ontario, Canada M4V 3B2
Penguin Books India (P) Ltd, 11 Community Centre, Panchsheel Park,
New Delhi – 110 017, India
Penguin Group (NZ), cnr Airborne and Rosedale Roads, Albany,
Auckland 1310, New Zealand
Penguin Books (South Africa) (Pty) Ltd, 24 Sturdee Avenue,
Rosebank 2196, South Africa

Penguin Books Ltd, Registered Offices: 80 Strand, London WC2R 0RL, England

www.penguin.com

First published 2004
2

Text copyright © Kay Woodward, 2004
Illustrations copyright © Strawberrie Donnelly, 2004
All rights reserved

The moral right of the author and illustrator has been asserted

Set in Weiss
Made and printed in England by Clays Ltd, St Ives plc

British Library Cataloguing in Publication Data
A CIP catalogue record for this book is available from the British Library

ISBN 0–141–31878–3

Contents

Welcome to the secret world of dolphins . . .

Which is your most favourite animal in the world? Is it a fluffy kitten? A tall, graceful giraffe? Or . . . is it the delightful, darling, dazzling dolphin?

Dolphins are found in oceans, seas, rivers and lakes – swimming deep below the surface, and flipping and twirling on the crest of a wave.

Sleek, speedy and very clever, they have charmed and astonished people for thousands of years. But how much do we really know about them? How do they communicate with each other? Can they spend minutes, hours or days underwater? How do they look after their babies?

Dive into the magical world of dazzling dolphins, to find the answers to these questions and to meet the stars of the sea . . .

Chapter One
All about dolphins

The turquoise seawater moves gently to and fro. Suddenly, a brisk breeze rushes past, ruffling the water into small waves. Then all is still. Until . . . whoosh! A gorgeous grey dolphin leaps out of the water. Gracefully, the beautiful animal twists in the air and then dives back into the sea, vanishing beneath the water with the tiniest of splashes. Ripples spread outwards . . . until all is calm once more.

A dolphin is a very special kind of animal. It lives in a watery world, just like a fish, but it breathes air, just like a cat or dog. For a dolphin, both air and water are vital. Without both, they would not survive. The dolphin makes the most of both worlds. Imagine being able to swim

beneath the water for minutes at a time, then shooting into the sunlight above. A dolphin can do this – and more!

A closer look

Some dolphins are large, others are small. Some are patterned, others are plain. But all dolphins have the same basic features.

Their long jaws hold a mouthful of sharp teeth – many more than a human. These rows of teeth come in handy for catching fish and other prey. The **beak** can be used as a battering ram to attack vicious enemies. BAM!

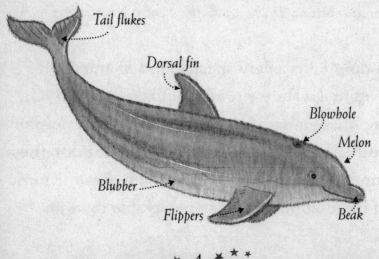

Tail flukes

Dorsal fin

Blowhole

Melon

Blubber

Flippers

Beak

Have you ever noticed the dolphin's rounded forehead? This fatty area is called a **melon** (really!). It works like a stereo speaker, sending the dolphin's clicks, whistles and high-pitched sounds through the water.

The **blowhole** on top of a dolphin's head is not just used for blowing — it's used for breathing too. Dolphins suck air through this hole when they are above water. When they dive, a flap of skin closes across the hole to make a watertight seal, in the same way as your eyelids shut tight to protect your eyes.

Swimming stars

Dolphins slide through water with the greatest of ease — their bodies are perfectly suited to swimming. They are streamlined, which means that their shape allows them to whizz through water. They are long and pointy, with no lumpy, bumpy or rough bits to slow them down.

The dolphin's **dorsal fin** sticks straight up. It

helps to keep the dolphin steady when it is swimming along. If you're dolphin spotting, this fin will be the very first clue that there are dolphins about . . .!

Flippers help the dolphin to turn, flip or dive in any direction. But it's the powerful muscles along the dolphin's back that make it rocket through the water. These move the tail up and down, to power the animal along. **Tail flukes** act just like the flippers that divers wear on their feet.

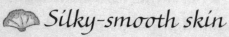

🐚 Silky-smooth skin

Dolphins have a very strict beauty routine to keep their skin as smooth as possible. But they

don't bother with cleansers, posh soaps or scrubs. Instead, they shed rough skin to reveal fresh, new, sleek skin beneath. This smooth skin helps the dolphin to slide through water at top speed.

Hidden under the dolphin's skin, there is a layer of fat, called **blubber**. This keeps it warm, even when the water is icy c-c-c-cold.

Water, water, all around

It is water that enables dolphins to move so quickly and gracefully. Water supports their weight as they swim, allowing them to move effortlessly. This is important for a heavy crea-ture like a dolphin – out of the water, a bottlenose dolphin can weigh as much as eight grown men!

Can you imagine what it must be like to be a dolphin? At the swimming pool or in the sea, float on your back and let the water hold you up. Then swim and glide through the water. Do

you feel as if you weigh nothing at all? That's why even the largest dolphins find it easy to move through water.

Dazzling dolphin secrets

⭐ Dolphins shed their skin every two hours!

⭐ Male swimmers sometimes shave their entire bodies to make sure that their skin is smooth, like a dolphin's. Hairy chests and legs would slow them down.

⭐ Dolphins are closely related to whales and porpoises. Whales are bigger and porpoises are smaller, but they all belong to the same family — cetaceans.

Chapter Two
A watery world full of dolphins

*I*n the cold waters of the North Atlantic Ocean, a
beautiful yellow, white and grey dolphin swims.
Nearby, a magnificent black and white dolphin surges
into the air. On the opposite side of the world, a
silvery dolphin with a long, pointed beak makes its
way along an Indian river. Dazzlingly different
dolphins live in the world's oceans, seas and rivers –
all unique, all beautiful!

There are thirty-seven different species of
dolphin – thirty-two of these spend most of
their lives swimming in salty seawater, although
they sometimes swim in fresh water. Some
species can only be found in one ocean, while
dolphins like bottlenoses can be found all over

the world. Some prefer to swim deep in the middle of the ocean. Others like to stay near the coast. There are five species that are river dolphins. They look different to their ocean-living cousins because they have long, pointed beaks and teeny tiny eyes. But whichever habitat they prefer, most dolphins have one particular area of sea, ocean or river that is home sweet home.

A river dolphin

🐚 A sea full of dolphins

If you sailed round the world, here are just a few of the dolphins you might be lucky enough to see . . .

Spinner dolphins

These dolphins have very long pointed beaks and flippers. Just like their name, they love to twirl, whirl and spin high in the air.

Rough-toothed dolphins

As their name suggests, they really do have rough teeth! They have fewer – but bigger – chompers than other dolphins, with lots of wrinkles in them.

Risso's dolphins

It's easy to recognize these dolphins because they have strange, white patterns on their bodies that look just like graffiti. They are actually scars from fights and accidents. The older the dolphin, the worse the 'graffiti'.

Common dolphins

There are millions of these dolphins all around the world. They are very noisy. You can sometimes

hear their high-pitched squeals from above the water. Underneath the surface, they must be deafening . . .

Bottlenose dolphin

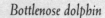

Bottlenose dolphin

The most famous dolphin of them all. Beautiful, grey, sleek and with a huge smile, this dolphin has been photographed more times and starred in more films and wildlife documentaries than any other. They often visit harbours and river estuaries, so you might be lucky enough to see one!

Orca or killer whale

The orca is the largest dolphin of all. This beautiful black and white creature is also known as the killer whale, but really it is a dolphin not a whale. Other large dolphins include melon-headed whales and pilot whales.

Orca

🐚 *Can you spot a dolphin?*

Some dolphins have weird and wonderful names. Can you guess which of the following dolphin names belong to real species?

1. Boto
2. Fraser's dolphin
3. Heaviside's dolphin
4. Hourglass dolphin
5. Irrawaddy dolphin
6. Southern right whale dolphin
7. Striped dolphin
8. Tucuxi

Answer

They're ALL real dolphins! Boto is a river dolphin from South America. Fraser's dolphin likes to swim in tropical places. Heaviside's dolphin lives in very small groups. Hourglass dolphin has a lovely bendy shape and black and white markings. Irrawaddy dolphin adores warm shallow water. Southern right whale dolphin has no fin! Striped dolphin has black, blue and white stripes. And Tucuxi can live in both salty and fresh water.

Dazzling dolphin secrets

The rarest dolphin in the world is the Baiji, which lives in the Yangtze River in China. If the river is dammed, which it may well be, the few remaining Baiji might vanish altogether.

The fin of a fully grown male killer whale can be as tall as a man!

 *Fully grown male dolphins are slightly longer than females and much heavier.*

Chapter Three
Living with dolphins

*I*n the distance, tiny white-capped waves are racing
along. Nearer and nearer they come, faster and
faster, until it's clear that these aren't waves at all –
they are dancing, prancing, splashing dolphins!
Countless dolphins are chasing along the surface of
the water. Then, as if they decide all at once that the
performance is over, they vanish beneath the waves.

Dolphins are friendly creatures – they like the
company of other dolphins. Although a few live
alone, most live together in groups called pods.
Dolphin pods can range in size from two to . . .
wait for it . . . thousands!

Sticking together . . . staying apart

Dolphin pods are not just made up of family members. Instead, females of the same and different families join together with their young. They all work as a team. The mums, aunts, cousins and sisters all rally round to help when calves are born – and often take turns in looking after the little ones as they grow older.

Male dolphins swim away from the females as soon as they are old enough. They make friends with the other young males and live with them. It is thought that male and female pods only get together to mate.

Touchy-feely dolphins

Dolphins have a very good sense of touch and use body contact in the same way as humans. A mother will rub a flipper against

her calf, perhaps to remind it to stay close.
Long-lost dolphin pals also rub their flippers
together, just as humans hug or kiss.

Sometimes, dolphins touch each other in an
angry way. If there is a fight, they will bite each
other, or bash each other with their flippers or
tails. Some of these fights are just for fun. Some
scuffles happen when two males decide that
they both like the same female dolphin . . .

Time to play

Dolphins are very playful creatures. They all
love to frolic, frisk and swim together – even
the grown-ups. Both younger and older
dolphins have even been spotted playing catch
– throwing seaweed back and forth – and chasing each other!

Groups of dolphins are often seen surfing
along on the crest of a wave – they don't need
wetsuits and surfboards like humans. And bow
riding is a real treat. When a boat powers

through the water, its bow – the front of the
boat – pushes a wave of water in front of it.
Dolphins hitch a free ride on this wave.
Wheeeeeeeeeeee!

Time to eat

The dolphins' magical underwater world is filled
with a never-ending supply of food. In the sea
there are fish, squid and jellyfish to eat, while
river dolphins feast on fish, crabs and clams.
When a dolphin meets a shoal of fish, it has a
very clever way of catching them. Just like a

shepherd and sheepdog round up a flock of sheep, the dolphin herds the fish, keeping them together. This makes it easier to catch enough fish for a dolphin-sized appetite.

But there are dangers under the water too. Enemies lurk beneath the waves, eager for a tasty bite. Dolphins must take care that they don't become a shark's next meal.

Dazzling dolphin secrets

 Pantropical spotted dolphins may live in pods as big as 3,000. These dolphins will never be short of friends!

No one is exactly sure how long dolphins live – it's hard to keep track of these speedy swimmers. Many think that the average age is around twenty-five. Some believe that a few dolphins may live as long as fifty years!

Dolphins are the gymnasts of the sea! They can dive really deep and then shoot upwards to leap high above the waves.

Chapter Four
Baby dolphins

*T*he baby dolphin looks around in wonder at the
dazzling watery colours. Wow! Where is he?
Everything is so floaty and so lovely and so blue . . .
Then he feels a gentle nudge – and then another. His
mother is pushing him with her beak. Nudge. There
she goes again! Nudge, nudge. The baby moves
upwards through its new watery world. Nudge. Up he
swims. Nudge. He speeds up until his head breaks the
surface and – aaaaah. Fresh air! He takes his first
breath.

Dolphin babies do not need many swimming
lessons. Straight after the birth, a mother
dolphin pushes and prods her baby upwards.
There is a very important reason for this. A

mother dolphin has to make sure that her baby dolphin – called a calf – knows where to find air and how to breathe.

When the baby dolphin reaches the surface of the water, it takes its very first gulp of fresh air. It is important that the calf learns this quickly – it will have to breath air every few minutes for the rest of its life.

Mothers and calves

Dolphins are mammals, like you and me. And, just like humans, dolphins give birth to babies rather than laying eggs, like fish or birds. A dolphin baby looks just like its mother when it's born, only much smaller.

A mother dolphin will have a calf every two or three years. Each calf stays by her side for the first year or two of its little life, until it is big enough and smart enough to survive on its own.

🐚 Staying close

In these first one or two years, the mother dolphin feeds her baby extra-rich milk, which is packed full of goodness. The milk is much

thicker and creamier than the sort you might find in your fridge — it helps the young dolphin to grow big, strong and healthy. A mother dolphin feeds her baby every few minutes right around the clock!

Zooming along

A baby dolphin has its own way of being 'carried' by its mother, just like a human baby. But instead of being lifted, it hitches a ride by staying very close to its mother's side while swimming. The mother does all the work of cutting through the water, and the baby stays in her slipstream, hardly moving a flipper. This way, the baby doesn't use up all its energy and get tired when travelling long distances.

By following its mother, a calf learns how to survive. When its mother dives, so does the calf. When she goes to the surface, the calf is there too. When she hunts for fish, the calf comes along to watch and learn how to hunt for itself.

Dazzling dolphin secrets

Baby dolphins do not suck milk like human babies. Their mothers squirt milk straight into their mouths!

To protect her calf from danger, a dolphin holds the baby close with her flippers.

When a calf is naughty, its mother butts it gently with her head. This reminds the baby dolphin to behave.

Chapter Five
Dozing dolphins

*T*he dolphin floats in the shallow water. Is it asleep or awake? Are its eyes open or closed? It's hard to tell. All around, ocean life carries on exactly as normal. Currents tug the water gently to and fro. Small fish swim past. Then, slowly, the dolphin appears to come back to life. Its eyes open fully and the beautiful creature glides away.

As mammals, dolphins need to breathe air every few minutes to survive. If they spent too long underwater they would drown. So, how do they sleep?

Dolphins have a very clever way of resting. Like humans, they spend about a third of their lives asleep. But, unlike humans, they never fall

fast asleep. Instead, they snooze . . .

🐚 Half asleep

To make sure it doesn't drown, a sleepy dolphin
uses the left and right sides of its brain in a very
special way. When we sleep our whole brain is
resting, but only half of a dolphin's brain sleeps
at a time. While it is semi-slumbering, the half
of the dolphin's brain that is awake knows
exactly what's going on, and is alert to danger. It
also stops the dolphin banging into anything,
such as a boat or a reef, and makes sure the
dolphin goes up to the surface to take a vital
breath of fresh air. After about two hours, it's

time for this half of the brain to rest, while the other half takes over the sleep duties!

Dolphins don't lie down to sleep on the seabed. Usually they doze while floating upright or horizontally, or they swim slowly beside another dolphin while staying half-asleep. They can also rest in shallow water.

Non-stop swimming

For the first few weeks of a dolphin's life, its mother never stays still to nap — she is always swimming. Very young dolphins do not have enough blubber to float easily, and if the mother dolphin did stop, the calf would sink. So, while her baby is still young, the mother dolphin snoozes as she swims. The calf catches a breath of air whenever its mum pops up to the surface.

In the middle of the night . . .

When it's dark, dolphins often fall into a deeper type of sleep, called 'logging'. They float near

the top of the water, with their blowholes above the surface. This way, they can sleep and breathe. It is known as 'logging', because the dolphins look like logs, floating on the water!

Dazzling dolphin secrets

When a bottlenose dolphin snoozes and the left-hand side of its brain falls asleep, the right eye closes. When the right-hand side of the brain sleeps, the left eye closes!

Dolphins have much bigger lungs than humans, so they can take much bigger breaths of air. This is one of the reasons why they take fewer breaths than humans and can stay under the water for minutes at a time.

No one knows whether or not dolphins dream. Maybe they dream of meeting or swimming with humans!

Chapter Six
Echo, echo, echo . . .

*T*he dolphin glides beneath the waves. Even though the water is murky and muddy, it knows exactly where it is going. A little to the right, then onwards it swims, towards its goal. Suddenly, through the gloom, a shoal of grey mullet appears. How did the dolphin find them? There's no time for questions – it's time for dinner.

Some dolphins have very good vision. Bottlenose dolphins can see a long way through air. They can also see long distances through clear water. But, mysteriously and magically, they can also find their way through the darkest and gloomiest of water – even in the middle of the night.

Ganges River dolphins have very bad eyesight; they are almost blind. But even though the water in the Ganges River is very murky, these dolphins find food, find their way – and survive.

So how do bottlenose dolphins, Ganges River dolphins and all other dolphins find out where they are? Why don't they get lost? The answer is echolocation.

Echolocation means finding out where objects are by using echoes. Although only a few types of dolphin have been shown to have this ability, scientists think that all dolphins may be able to echolocate.

How does echolocation work?

First, a dolphin makes clicking noises in its nasal cavities. The clicks are very high-pitched, so they don't get confused with the lower sounds that dolphins use to communicate.

Next, the clicking sound travels through the

dolphin's melon at the front of its head. The melon concentrates all these clicks into a narrow beam of sound that travels forward through the water. When the clicking sound hits an object, some sound is bounced back as an echo to the dolphin. It doesn't 'hear' the sound with its ear, but through its jaw!

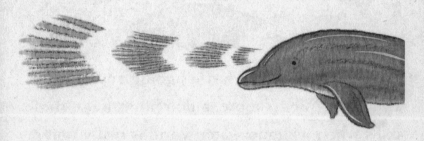

Here's the really clever part: the time the click took to travel to the object and back tells the dolphin how far away it is! The dolphin swims forward, sending out clicks and receiving click echoes as it goes. It can even tell which direction the sound is coming from, depending on which side of its jaw receives more of the echo.

🐚 Special skills

Even more amazing is that these clever creatures can tell exactly what an object is, even though they cannot see it! The click echoes that bounce off an object back to the dolphin reveal many things – the size of the object, which direction

it's travelling in, how fast it's going and how far away it is. What's more, a dolphin can use these skills when its underwater world is really noisy. They can communicate with other dolphins while they are echolocating. And they can even detect different objects – that may be near and far away – at the same time.

To get an idea of how difficult this is, try to imagine listening to the radio while the TV is on, your mum is talking loudly on the phone and the dog is barking – all in the same room!

Dazzling dolphin secrets

Sound travels much faster underwater than it does above the waves. Dolphins' brains have to work very quickly to decode the echo information that whizzes back through the water to them.

Some people say that a female dolphin can sense when a female diver is pregnant, using her echolocation skills. It is said that dolphins have been known to protect a pregnant diver and her unborn baby.

Like dolphins, bats have excellent echolocation skills. But, unlike dolphins, they use these to find tasty insects and to make sure they don't crash into cave walls at night.

Chapter Seven
Whistles and clicks

*T*he mother dolphin sends out a special whistle to her brand-new calf. Over and over she whistles. Soon the baby dolphin will recognize her call. He will be able to hear his mother, even when the sounds of other dolphins are all around. It's a sound he'll never forget.

Dolphins make a huge range of noises, including whistles, squeaks, moans, grunts, trills and clicks. They sometimes sound like creaking doors! Dolphins make noises for two important reasons. The first is echolocation, their special way of finding food, each other and their way around. The second is communication – dolphins like to talk to each other!

A mysterious language

For years, people have eagerly listened to the noises dolphins make. Many believe that they have a special language all of their own. Does this language contain words, like human languages? Does it contain warning sounds, friendly sounds and angry sounds? No one knows for sure, but dolphins do seem to pass information between each other. They also make noises when a fellow dolphin returns to the pod, as if they are welcoming it back.

If dolphins really do have their own language, maybe one day we'll be able to work out what they are saying. Do they shout with delight as they ride waves? Do they whisper secrets to each other?

Do they gossip about humans? If we discover what their magical and mysterious whistles and clicks mean, it is possible that one day we may be able to have a conversation with them. How amazing would that be?

Clever dolphins?

Dolphins can be trained to perform amazing tricks and complicated tasks. They can find and track a shoal of fish, even in the murkiest water. Does this mean they are as clever as us – if not more so?

Dolphins' brains are among the largest in the animal kingdom — a bottlenose dolphin's brain is bigger than a human brain. So maybe there is more to discover about their skills and intelligence, or maybe, as some people think, so much of the dolphin's brain is used for echolocation and communication that there isn't room for much more. But perhaps dolphins are incredibly clever creatures. Maybe they are clever enough to keep their intelligence a secret from humans? I believe that. Do you?

Dazzling dolphin secrets

⭐ Many of the signals that dolphins send out are far too high to be heard by humans. The very high sounds are used for finding their way, while lower sounds are used for communication.

⭐ Unlike most other animals, dolphins can recognize their own reflection in a mirror!

⭐ If there is danger, dolphins work as a team.

Chapter Eight
Dazzling dolphins

*L*ong ago, there was a Greek musician named Arion, who sang and played like an angel. Arion entered a famous musical competition and was delighted to win huge riches. He bought a boat and sailed off to enjoy his prize. But the crew of his boat wanted Arion's riches for themselves. So they captured him and gave him a choice – he could die at their hands, or they would throw him into the sea. Shocked at this betrayal, Arion chose the sea. But first, he dressed in his finest robes and played a haunting melody on his lyre. From all around, sea creatures gathered to listen. And, when the musician was hurled beneath the waves, a dolphin was waiting to rescue him. Arion was carried safely to shore by the heroic creature.

This Greek myth is one of the many wonderful stories about dolphins that have been told over the centuries. The Ancient Greeks worshipped the dolphin – they believed that it was the god Apollo. The Romans also held dolphins in great awe. Archaeologists have found coins, pottery and walls decorated with dolphins. There are intricate mosaics of leaping dolphins, swimming

dolphins and a dolphin with Cupid, the god of love, perched on its back!

And dolphins are just as popular today. Tales of dolphin daring and bravery amaze and

astound all who hear them. Perhaps this is one of the reasons why people are so fascinated by these creatures . . .

Stars of the sea

Dolphins have appeared in countless nature programmes and documentaries. Thousands of books have been written about them. They have even starred in movies.

Flipper (1996) is a film about an orphaned dolphin that befriends a young boy. Together, they have a splashtastic adventure! Not one, but four dolphins played the part of Flipper. Three of the Flippers were beautiful bottlenose dolphins, while the fourth was a robot!

🪷 Celebrity dolphin

On the west coast of Ireland, there lives one of the world's most famous dolphins. Funghi the dolphin swims near the entrance to Dingle Bay, County Kerry. He is the biggest tourist attraction in Dingle – people visit him from all over the world. The friendly bottlenose dolphin often swims alongside the boats in the harbour, but can sometimes be spotted from the water's edge. Funghi made his first appearance in 1983. No one knows how much longer it will be before he vanishes forever.

🐚 A trusty guide

Set within the coastline of New Zealand, there is a dangerous channel of water called Pelorus Sound. Many ships have been shipwrecked while trying to sail here. But, over a hundred years ago, a helpful dolphin came to the rescue. The Risso's dolphin, who became known as Pelorus Jack, guided vessels safely through the hazardous waters. It is said that between 1888 and 1912, not a single ship sank in Pelorus Sound.

🐚 Dolphin lifeguards

There are countless stories of dolphins who have saved swimmers and sailors from drowning. One extraordinary event happened in 2000 . . . A young boy fell overboard from his father's boat near the south coast of Italy. No one saw him tumble into the sea – except Filippo, the local bottlenose dolphin. Filippo nudged the boy above the waves, urging him to hang on to

his fin. But that's not all. Filippo then pushed the boy back towards the boat, near enough for his father to drag him back to safety.

Dazzling dolphin secrets

Funghi is the Italian word for mushroom. What an odd name for a dolphin!

When a dolphin is in danger, other dolphins will rush to the rescue with no thought of danger to themselves.

Dolphins never get sore eyes from salty seawater. Their eyes are filled with special oily tears that protect them.

Chapter Nine
Dolphins and people

The sunlight glints on the turquoise water. A girl stands, waiting. Then, as if by magic, a sleek, grey fin rises, slicing through the water's surface. A friendly face appears and opens its jaws to show the biggest smile in the ocean. The dolphin makes a clicking noise, as if signalling the girl to catch hold. And she does, wrapping her eager fingers round the dolphin's fin. Then – they're off!

Many people have been lucky enough to swim with dolphins. The gentle creatures circle close to the swimmers, indicating their willingness to be touched. The dolphins then take them for a ride or nudge them playfully. It is one of the greatest experiences ever!

Although some of these dolphins live in captivity, more and more dolphin swims are taking place in the wild. The dolphins are free to come and go as they please.

Dolphins in danger

It may seem hard to believe, but even though people love dolphins, they are the dolphins' biggest enemies. Humans catch lots of fish, leaving fewer for dolphins to eat. People also

pollute the sea, so the food that dolphins eat is poisoned. When rivers are dammed, river dolphins have fewer places to live.

Drilling from oil rigs and other loud noises confuse dolphins. The sounds can interfere with their echolocation skills.

Wild and free

Although many dolphins have been taken from the wild to perform for crowds of people, these shows are becoming much less popular. People prefer to see dolphins dazzling in their natural habitat rather than jumping through hoops at the toot of a whistle. And that's just what they can do at dolphin sanctuaries around the world!

At the Shark Bay Marine Nature Reserve in Australia, friendly dolphins can drop in when they feel like it. This is a place where humans

can come close to dolphins and where no creature is harmed. The dolphins circle curious
animal lovers, nudging and nuzzling them.
Then, when they've had enough, they swim
away.

Dolphin therapy

Many people believe that dolphins can heal
humans. There are amazing stories of children
speaking for the first time after swimming with
dolphins. These calming creatures appear to
cure depression too.

Whether it's because their
smiling faces give people a
boost, whether swimming
with dolphins makes
people relax, or whether
dolphins have a secret,
hidden power, nobody
knows. But, magically and
wonderfully, it seems to work . . .

Dazzling dolphin secrets

If you want to make sure that the tuna you are eating has been caught without harming dolphins (which sometimes swim near tuna shoals and get caught in the fishing nets), look on the side of the tin. There will be a short message or a picture of a happy dolphin.

After a wild dolphin gave his son the ride of his life, one doctor became fascinated by these wonderful creatures. Dr Horace Dobbs has now written many books about their ability to heal the sick and to give people hope.

In 2003, thousands of people were asked which special thing they'd most like to do in their lifetime. Was it travelling around the world? Was it dancing with the Royal Ballet? Was it diving on the Great Barrier Reef? No! Swimming with dolphins was the number-one choice!

Chapter Ten
A magical dolphin world

*I*f you love dolphins, why not create your own dolphin bedroom? It will be your very own oasis of calm. And with dazzling sea creatures all around, you might even dream of dolphins here!

Top tip: remember to ask Mum or Dad for help, or at least get their permission before splashing dye or paint anywhere!

Dazzling dolphin duvet cover

Do you have a faded old duvet cover that you'd like to brighten up? Here's what you need to transform it into a dazzling dolphin duvet . . .

* A sheet of tracing paper * A pencil
* A piece of card   * A pair of scissors
* Dark-blue fabric paint

A dolphin stencil

First, make a stencil following the outline on the next page like this . . .

1. Place the tracing paper over the outline and trace the dolphin shape with your pencil.
2. Flip the tracing paper over and scribble over the dolphin outline.
3. Now flip the tracing paper back and place it on top of the card. Using your pencil, trace over the dolphin line again, pressing quite firmly.
4. When you lift the tracing paper off – ta daaaaa! – the dolphin outline will have trans-ferred itself on to the card. To complete your stencil, all you need to do is ask an adult to cut out the dolphin shape.

Dazzling design

Decide what type of dolphin design you will follow before you start. Here are some ideas:

★ Dolphins placed at random all over the cover.
★ A pod of dolphins swimming across the middle of the cover.
★ A heart-shaped outline of dolphins.
★ An even better idea of your own!

Paint-tastic!

Make sure the duvet cover is nice and flat on a protected surface. Then, following your design, place the stencil on top. Now you're ready to paint over the stencil with your fabric paint – but make sure that you keep it totally still. When you remove the stencil, a perfect dolphin will be swimming across your duvet!

Why not use different colours for your dolphins? If you have a darker duvet cover, silver dolphins would look really magical.

Top tip: remember to follow the instructions on the fabric paint carefully to make sure that your dolphins stay exactly where you painted them. You don't want them to swim away during the night . . .

Underwater world

If you've ever watched a home makeover programme you'll know that a lick of paint can make all the difference to a room. So why not use a dolphin theme to decorate your walls? Here's what you need . . .

* Light-blue paint
* Paintbrushes
* Dark-blue paint
* A dolphin stencil
* And the most important thing of all – dust sheets!

1. First, tidy your room! (Don't worry, the other instructions are much more exciting.) Next, put dust sheets over your bed, bookshelves and all carpets and furniture. Now you're ready to start!

2. Draw a rough wavy line round the room – about a third of the way down from the ceiling – with a pencil. This will be the surface of the sea.

3. Paint the wall above the line light blue. Make sure that you go a little way over the wavy line. This light blue will be the sky.

4. After making sure that the light-blue paint is dry, paint right up to the line with the dark-blue paint. The crests of the waves could be very dramatic!

5. When you're done, wait a few hours while everything dries. To avoid paint fumes, it might be best to camp out in the living room for a night.

When the paint is dry . . .

Choose some dazzling paint for your dolphin
decorations. Silver paint would work well – and
would look really magical by lamplight! Or you
could try other glittery or light shades of paint.
As long as it stands out from the dark water, it
will look lovely!

Using the stencil from page 54, carefully
paint dolphins all over your wall. Some might
be swimming under the water. Others might be
leaping above the waves – whooooosh!

Dolphin calm

To make your magical dolphin world complete, play a recording of relaxing dolphin sounds and music in your room. All you'll need is a small tape recorder . . . and your imagination!

Get your tape recorder and find some sounds that are like dolphin clicks and whistles. Here are some ideas to start you off.

* Waves (if you live beside the seaside)
* Water rushing around the washing machine (if you don't)
* Clicking, snapping fingers
* Soft, haunting notes on a recorder
* The plucking of a guitar string
* Echoes

Once you've made your recording, press 'play', lie back, close your eyes and listen. If you're lucky, you'll dream of dolphins . . .